Note to Self

Note to Self

Poems by

Anastasia Vassos

Cover design by Shay Culligan
Cover art: Fountain Paris ©Gary Koeppel 2011
www.garykoeppel.com
Feather pen image by Da Vector on Unsplash
Author photo by Donna Vassos

ISBN: 979-8-90146-851-7
Library of Congress Control Number: 2026937247

Kelsay Books
502 South 1040 East, A-119
American Fork, Utah 84003
Kelsaybooks.com

For George Kalogeris
role model, mentor, friend
with gratitude

Acknowledgments

My thanks to the editors of the following journals in which these poems appeared, sometimes in alternate versions:

Comstock Review: "The day Jack Gilbert kissed me," "Worth"
Diode Poetry Journal: "It Could Be Any Day, Say, January 11," "Made Manifest"
Eunoia Review: "Note to Self: Ars Poetica," "Note to Self: River," "Note to Self: Other Side" (published as "Note to Self: Transformation"), "Note to Self: Undeterred"
Intima, A Journal of Medicine: "Architecture of Anatomy" (nominated for Pushcart Prize)
Kelsay Books' Women's Poetry Contest: "October" (honorable mention, 2023)
Lily Poetry Review: "Letter to Peter the Priest as He Awaits the Day of Judgment"
Mason Street Review: "The Poet Goes About Her Business"
Muriel Craft Bailey Poetry Contest: "Worth" (special merit, 2025)
Nature of Our Times: "Lake Waban"
New Verse News: "The Sun Shines Through the Venetian Blinds" (published as "Russia Invades Ukraine")
Nixes Mate Review: "Ode to My Spleen"
NOSTOS (Kelsay Books, 2023): "Dear God"
ODYSSEY.PM: "How I Became Bilingual," "Nepenthe," "Reading George Kalogeris's Poetry, I Remember My Mother's Grape Leaves"
Passager Journal Poetry Contest: "Dear God" (finalist, 2022)
Pensive Journal: "Stick Season"
Quartet Journal: "In the Way"

Red Letter Poems: "Letter to God, Just in Case"
RHINO: "Standing in Line at the Post Office, I Want to Mail My Book to My Dead Mother"
Small Orange: "I can say that"
Soundings East, Salem State University: "Letter to the Driver of the White SUV That Killed a Crow"
Taos Journal of Poetry: "October"
Thrush Poetry Journal: "Reading Jane Hirshfield at 6AM," "Thessaloniki, 1970" (nominated for Best of the Net)
Triggerfish Critical Review: "My Mariana Trench"
WCAI Radio Poetry Sunday: "The Three Sisters"
Whale Road Review: "November"
Willows Wept: "Garden State"

And enormous gratitude:

To Karen Kelsay and Olivia Loftis for guiding *Note to Self* toward publication. To Jennifer Barber, Suzanne Mercury, and Kyle Potvin for their generous blurbs.

To teachers who provided guidance and inspiration for some of these poems: Marie Howe, Amanda Moore, Laurie Wagner. Heartfelt gratitude to Mark Doty for all I've learned, and for giving me the idea for this book.

To Tuesday Night Poets: Diane Alters, Katherine Gekker, Vance Hedderel, Barbara Johnstone, Susan Miller, Joyce Schmid, Laura Paul Watson, and Connie Zumpf. To the Darlings: Shirley Brewer, Emily Buchanan, Anne Canright, Tracey O'Rourke, Carol Tell. To Amanda's Muses: Phyllis Klein, Kathy Les, Mistee St. Clair, Renee Schell, Catherine Wald, and Abby Wheeler. To Frances Donovan, and Sarah Dickenson Snyder.

To Eileen Cleary, Richard Foerster, and Melissa Green for their keen edits to this manuscript.

Shout out to Kristin Korten Brown and Barbara Cornwell Holt for liking my poems no matter what, every week.

My love to the best sister, Donna Vassos. To the man of my dreams and the love of my life Gary Koeppel, with whom all things are possible.

Contents

Made Manifest

I can barely stand without flinching.
Scorched Earth, you scorch
more than last July.
This spring, the forsythia refused
their gold before greening.
All that.
The light lingers
lasts and lasts
just doesn't stop.
How can it be
I'm afraid of the dark
afraid to die
and yet this incessant light?
Something under my skin
needs repair.
I couldn't stand it in Sweden
midsummer, revelry lasting until 3
and still no dark.
I like to shut things down
put things away, the clothes, the day.
At night, I can close my eyes, make my own dark
where phosphenes twirl
trapping the night air.
Morning, I regard Boston's toothy skyline
from the safety of my porch
the city's grimacing smile
the day's first sun pouring
as my thoughts erupt.
Ebb and flow, shudder and know.
I stand at the brink of my life

my hand cupped over my brow.
I regard the ocean's distant harbor
wind tossing through my skin.
I am *not* losing it, that sense
of where I'm going.
I've merely lost sight of it
temporarily. Every word I utter
has been used over and over.
If I repeat a word often enough
it loses
or maybe gains meaning:
last last last
and so on.
And so on.
When I was 13,
I wrote
the last leaf floated to the ground
like a feather.
A feather.

Note to Self: Ars Poetica

Something off course. Something on.

Thunder underneath.

The hummingbird sipping bougainvillea
inside my chest.

This one. This hummingbird.

Dear God,

I saw you today in the grocery store
stacking pomegranates. I recognized your dreadlocks.

I saw you holding my *American Heritage Dictionary*
page 48 searching all the words with Greek roots.

There you were in the maple tree's phalanges
the blaring canopy grounded

wet leaves and the grass
stunted by November's cheek.

At 4am you appeared behind my eyelids
in the shape of a boat—was that on purpose?—

—struts and joints and ribs
and stretchers almost shining.

Thank you for my body. Thank you for listening
to my babbling until an hour before dark.

In the park, the Orthodox priest passes
floating on his cloud of faith

his black cassock, cylindrical hat
long and tall. I wipe dust off my shoe.

I thought that was you, in the soot on my finger
after I passed it through the candle flame.

Dear God,

when you see me eating in church
it’s because I hunger.

Garden State

That madman Apollo
drags past the Meadowlands,
and across the Hudson
New York City splays her silver-steel
like the Mother of Them All.

It's October, the sun burns
its pat of butter on the air.
Here, the canopies of the northern red oak bloom
glorious spring-green crowns
while up north Persephone has teethed
her pomegranate seeds
and Boston's graying maples have shut down
their fingered leaves.

New Jersey—perfect balance
between industrial head and earth-churned heart—
we ride past the teeming wetlands
past the Hackensack River and its beauty
past Troy Meadows and Parsippany, their freshwater marshes
past the landfill that exudes its open scent
past the leaking oil tanks underground
along Tonnelle Avenue in North Bergen
past Newark's contaminated estuaries and ground-level ozone.

At first I thought I'd have to memorize
this poem that praises the kidney-shaped state,
lauds fall foliage, eulogizes the Greeks
and their crazy gods.

The four of us in the car
haven't eaten since morning
so no one speaks
as we try to get home in this rush.

A black Cadillac passes us on the right—
the side-mirror an inch from ours
the hiss of tires on asphalt—
and narrowly misses us.

My brother-in-law drives for his living
and though he's doing 80
in a 65-mile zone and everyone else is doing 90
I tell myself
we're in his good, capable hands.

The gods wail in their solitude
on the high mountain, Olympus
squatting in a distance
we may never reach—down here
in this adjacent state
that holds the most people in America
everyone is racing. Everyone.
I won't die in traffic today,
I won't go hungry tonight.
And the sun is shining
like there's no tomorrow.

Worth

How the painting's yellow wash pulls me
to my mother
because she loved yellow.

How I thought of God this morning
as I pedaled my bicycle past the ocean
I love best—

wondering whether I'm foolish to pray—
sand sifting
this flash of wanting.

It's so small, almost not worth writing about
the pale monarch resting
in the middle of the walk leading to the house—

my hand next to it, palm up
the butterfly crawling to clutch my finger—
how I placed her on the fading hydrangea
next to the door, how she stayed for hours

the sun glimmering, the paint still wet.

Rolling Prairie

I cross the line
from Michigan
into Indiana pedaling 15 mph
maybe slower
up the rolling hills
at the summit of one
I stop.
Breathing hard. The clipping
from the pedals, muted.

The cows lie in their pen
shaded by three yellow poplars
the mud cradling their swollen bellies.
My GPS tells me I've arrived
in Rolling Prairie in another state
high on this hill
and once my breathing calms
I hear nothing—
nothing but the breathing
of these Brown Swiss Dairy's
that for a minute
I don't recognize
as cows
the color of mud.
I have never seen
cows like these
mothers full of milk
resting and one calf stands up.

When did I leave Michigan?
Where did I cross over?

I used to think
the only place in the world
that hushed
complete silence
was that tiny island
in the middle of the Aegean
her winding roads
leading up to Volax Village
to giant boulders
placed along the cliffs
harboring stillness where I felt
myself alone in the world.
Everyone who made me feel young
is gone now—
my mother and her sisters, my father
my ancient lineage
a chain worn
but not broken.
I clip into the bike
and continue—
both sides
of the Atlantic
my parents born near water
in Asia Minor

now buried
underground in America's middle west
their silence
not exactly like that road
to Volax Village
or Rolling Prairie
but like that.

I can say that

the first sound was singing.
The second was Greek.
Before that Elytis, Seferis
before that Sappho, singing—
before that Homer.

Here's what I remember:
sitting at my mother's feet
to learn the Orthodox
plea of faith
syllable by syllable.

I can say that my first word was no.

It's 6am in Cincinnati—
how I sigh
as I write these words—
how I hold my breath.

I can say that I recited six Greek
words for love,
one Greek name for maker—
I recited prayers in reverse:
before that, declaration.
Faith. And no faith.

As though my breath were a syllable
I could not lose.
Then came singing.
Then comes yes.

Santiago Compostela Cathedral

It takes eight men in hightops and red robes
bending their knees
tightening their bellies
pulling ropes to sway the weight
of the silver thurible,
its burden suspended from a fixed pivot
by common rope.
Incense rises in the shape of a dove
up to heaven's eternity,
if there is such holy precinct.

The faithful stand behind railings
to keep them safe
from getting hit by the thing.
They've settled their dusty pilgrimage,
having had enough of wooden pillows
and supplication—
instead they hold up their phones
to the cathedral's ceiling
to record the thick incense cloud
as proof their prayers make it
up to God.
They shift their weight
on the bones of St. James.

Everyone wants to believe.

In Sunday school, Mrs. Papadopoulos
taught us how God made Adam
then took one of Adam's ribs to make Eve.
I placed my palm against my cage to feel the extra rib.
She said that's why women have one to spare.
Seven decades on this earth
and I believed that until yesterday.

Stick Season

The sun's dying pours
yellow pigment in the foyer
and douses the stairway
leading up to intimate rooms.

We have called this building
home for as long
as we've known
this city on the Atlantic.

Carnations in a glass vase
incandescent on the credenza.

When I was small, I stood
before the iconostasis
and prayed to Virgin Mary
that I wouldn't die.

I begged to ascend into heaven
the way she did, riding
on a chariot into eternal light.

I grip my coat
tight against evening.

October’s last leaves clutch
the oak’s branches

and the rhododendron reaches
above me, just as years
have stretched past
my skin, my bones.

I will call prayer
by another name: moonlight,
overcoat, night without stars.

Standing in Line at the Post Office, I Want to Mail My Book to My Dead Mother

she'd love these poems
I didn't write about her
all are about her

blood of my words

the ancient Greeks believed ichor
a fluid that lives forever
flowed in the veins
of their gods

it rained on such dry soil last night
the petrichor rose up
from dusty rocks

what is nostalgia
but a keen sense
of smell

I look out the dusty window
the sun is pouring oil
across the face of buildings
        I'm next in line

when my mother was dying
I read her Jane Hirshfield, Gwendolyn Brooks
that poem she loved by Lorenzo Mavilis

after I finished she looked at me
oh beautiful   her syllables like votives

I try to remember my Greek
I reach the counter   mail the book
the smell of blood rising up

Note to Self: River

My father was a river.
Mother, a river.
Upstream the ancestors watched
and I, a branch, a rock
along the thunderous way
reached for what was present
round every bend.
I remember this.

Letter to Peter the Priest as He Awaits the Day of Judgment

If you see Aunt Helen tell her
I still have the gold hoop earrings.
If you see my parents tell them I'm sorry.
My spine has herniated its disc
and I wake in the middle of the night, askew.
I wear socks to bed.
But why am I telling the dead
something they already know?
Show me the profile of Jesus
on this morning's burnt toast, the Facebook
post of the horse you rode in on
the boat that carried you out.
Show me the coffee grounds at the bottom
of the cup, prophesy my future:
the long journey through the mountains
the stranger I'll meet who'll bestow a gift.
In the Alaskan rain forest
my friend Mistee cared for her dying father
who kept smoking even as he lay
in the unmade bed.
After he died he sent her a crown
of sonnets. I won't ask
if God exists, though I'm curious—
when I pray I'll name you instead—
dear Petros, dear Rock.
Yes. I believe naming is praying.
Though you once said
you are not a man of faith,

I think that was just the blink of your eye—
your hands and heart witnesses
that Christ died for you.
Tell me about the afterlife:
do you still wear the collar? Those shiny clerical robes?
Do you have a body?
Have you met St. Demetrios?
Find out if St. George is still slaying the dragon,
his horse bucking under him.
Here in Boston winter has slid
into habit, hurling rain and shadow
shadow and rain instead of snow.
The virus lingers, mutates.
I'm left with the lamentation of the sky.
I'm left with two gold coins I forgot
to place on your eyelids when you fled.
Tell me: is there really a river?

It Could Be Any Day, Say, January 11

When he says Miscanthus is the state flower of New Jersey I think he's kidding until he tells me he remembers Chinese Silver Grass scattered over the Meadowlands back in the day. Feathery heads unfurled in winter's weak sun this Thursday morning walk—I shiver in the wind and this talk of childhood memories reminds me I am old. I had been thinking about my mother. What is it about remembering dementia? How she lost her thought—how I misplaced my phone three times today. My laptop invisible under the pile of papers. Why did I walk into this room? My brain this morning, back lit, wind moving through—misplaced thoughts scattered. My mother's classically-constructed mind so pristine once, so exact before it fractured. I've heard about the munitions explosion during the siege of Athens—the Venetian bomb nearly destroying the Parthenon's perfect curves. When I was small she taught me ancient Greek prayers I memorized, my brain an elastic band. And now? I want to believe I will not forget—that I don't harbor the spark that ignited her at the end. What is it about Miscanthus? Silver remnants surviving this harsh climate, white fruiting heads swaying even in winter. She had to let all that go, finally—debris scattered at her feet. She had no choice.

Ode to My Spleen

Little Blood Purifier.
Everything inside my body
is what I cannot see.
I surrender my laughter: infectious.
The white flag of my open palm.
Can you explain penance?
The lifeline that haunts the surface?
Melancholic Wonder. Absolver.
O body. O bold: define faith.
The circumference of love. Is it the size of a fist?
God. The birth of Polaris.
The beach where Achilles wept.

Architecture of Anatomy

I remind myself there's no dying
without living
as the techs slide me into the metal coffer
to see the compromised pillar of my spine.

The machine realigns the water molecules of my fragile
    scaffolding—
bone, muscle, ligaments rinsed clean in magnetic resonance
the shifts in frequency
sirens in the room—

I am tied to the mast
a doppler wave washes over my body
and somewhere an opera tenor joins the cacophony.
Is that a bend in the light?

An image tomorrow will show how my discs
resemble the ruins of a temple.

I want my body's Doric order restored—
like that strongest of columns in the Parthenon
before the explosion.

Reading Jane Hirshfield at 6AM

After the rain all night, Jane crosses my silent path
to continue hers.
I follow her across the room
to reach the lamp—
turn it on, turn it off, turn it on.
The quiet light
puddles the floor.
I gather my skirt in my two hands
lifting the folds
to keep the hem dry, then change
my mind letting the fabric
fall into the damp.

Daughters of Poseidon

The Aegean reaches for shore
desperate to retreat. It's so hot I can see
the heat rise centigrade
by dry centigrade.
My mother and her sisters
still sleep. The fisherman calls
down the dusty road.
Kellogg's Greek cornflakes
melt in milk.
I gulp the sweetness.

*

Before she fell
Aunt Helen was crazy for swimming.
When Greeks invite us to swim
they say   ας κάνουμε ένα μπάνιο—*let's take a bath*
they step gingerly into the Aegean—
up to their shoulders
heads above the surface—for hours.
Unlike other Greeks Helen swam
with her head down
she stroked and kicked the sea.

*

When I suggest we go for a swim
my sister doesn’t answer.
We stand at a pay phone
in Polyhrono Village. She dials
the number of her ex-boyfriend in California
who has stopped speaking to her.
She leaves a fourth message. A film of salt on our skin.
Maybe it’s the fifth message. The saddest walk
back to the house.
The Aegean lapping at our feet.

The Three Sisters

I see their trunks clearly
through the back window—
three sturdy birches
in my neighbor's yard
full of marrow
grieving tall and breathing.
I call them the three sisters—
like Orion's belt, Chekhov's play
those mountains in the Cascades.

*

The birch bark in my path
when I walked the woods
this morning? I picked it up—
found it full of portent—
those transverse streaks
on tree-skin as thin as my fingernail—
why do these woody contours
so remind me of the shape of a girl?

Lake Waban

It was always at dusk
that we would pile in the car
drive to the lake—
take off our clothes to swim—

the lake waves panting
and a loon—landing
on the surface
its flickering wail—
before ducking below—

how my body
in the soft water, the lake
calm, the silk of it
the closest I ever came
to being alone in the presence
of others—the night
coming up alive
crickets chirping down to sleep—
the wind meeting the branches
of the evergreens—the hum
of waves sweeping the shore.

It’s been almost 50 years.
We’re all still alive except Patrice.
The way the tributaries of her hair
splayed across the surface
of the water as she lay back—
as she floated above the ink-black depth.

Note to Self: Empty Room

Remind me what it's like to live
without poetry.
To ride the city train
head slung against the window
wet, black branches
straining the sky's veil.
Asymmetric clouds, descending.
To squeeze smoke out the gap
of a colorless flame.
Remind me
how the mouth goes mute.
Then, remind me
to enter an empty room
for the sake of knowing it—
remind me of six Greek words for love.

A Poet Goes About Her Business

Next door, little Isla names
the *one-eyed Susans* by the fence—
those late summer broods, petals
sunstruck for weeks.

The catalog offers seeds
like treats bound to my very edges:
wild geranium, slender dayflower
fragrant water lily.

I am not sad to be old today.
I can almost smell next year's
Nymphea odorata.

My Mariana Trench

Yesterday in my garden,
I shoved the shovel's blade
into earth and hit rock.

And on my walk, cold wind blew
and my eyes began to water.
I thought of nothing, kept walking, my handkerchief

lifting and dropping, lifting and dropping
as I dabbed at my tearing vision.
Blurry streetscape as if under water—

when I die, I want to be buried there
in the Mariana Trench, my love, with you—
to plumb a mystery we long for and refuse.

Before language brought us a word for *blue*
Homer described the sea *wine-dark.*
Let's agree *blue* can mean

sea or *bother* or *door* or *sky* . . .
don't the Greeks have so many words
for love: *agape, philia, storge, eros* . . .

wild trench deeper than Everest
is tall, darker than all I have to measure it by.

Angled Light

Standing up tall
in the high-collared vase
the tulips I bought this morning
from the grocery store.
Bright butter-yellow petals
please me—yellow—
my mother's favorite color
before she dwindled to earth.

Defiant green leaves
pierce the sun-filled shape
of the tulips' heads, caress them
as if they have the right to be
just as beautiful.

Sometimes I think
there's no use praying to God.
Rumi said anything you lose
comes round in another form.
I think he meant no need to grieve.
These tulips suffice.

The Sun Shines Through the Venetian Blinds

Instead of listening to news of the war
G puts on music to paint by—the scene of the Maine sunset
he took a photo of last summer.

The sun drops onto the dining room table
where I write. When my phone lights up,
it's Kristin in Kalamazoo, texting me

that her daughter-in-law's parents
have fled Kyiv to Zanzibar, that the children's hospital
where Natasha saved other lives has been bombed.

This small world verging on world war
when we thought world wars no longer possible.
I pick up the phone to call Kristin, she tells me
her daughter-in-law wept last night for her parents,

for their safety. Almost sadder than death.
I want to believe there is life after death,
that the good guys will win. The sun detonates through
the south-facing window on this last day of February.

The blasts in that faraway country do not discriminate.
It might be us: civilians under siege sleeping in subway
    stations.
Here, the sun keeps bombing.

Here's what I want you to know: the sun, as I sit
facing the window, explodes into my eyes as it sets.
If I move my head I won't be blinded.

Note to Self: Undeterred

On my knees

I dig in mud
in the gap
between the call
and response
of birds—

my mouth
an empty vowel.

One-in-a-Million Yellow Cardinal
Has Been Seen

A yellow cardinal alights
on my spine
somewhere between L5 and S1.

Small freak lands softly
and stays, its weight bearable
then not.

Odd creature
missing the enzymes
of its red cousins

pecks at bone
scratches at muscle
torments the perfect order

of Doric vertebrae.
As though the tree.
As though the branch, broken.

Archetype of dis-ease
drawn from the mind of God
and when I say *mind*

I mean wind
and when I say *God*
I mean dust.

Letter to God, Just in Case

What I mean to say is
I'm lonely. I haven't been praying.
I forgot to pray in February
and I'm sorry—
if you're there, you probably know
it's March now—light wanders past 5pm.
The hummingbird in my chest
sputters against my sternum
looking for a way out.
I read yesterday there's more evidence
for reincarnation
than for your existence—
this makes me question who I am.

How does it feel to watch us suffer?
Just last night a child was abducted
in a stolen car north of here.
She was wearing a pink coat.
I don't know how
to pray, it seems all I do is ask for stuff.
We are killing each other down here—
some of us in your name.
What I mean to say is
we're lonely and we all have regrets.

Send a sign: flick the lights on and off for a second
leave a shiny dime on the table
please find the little girl
in her pink coat
and return her to her parents.
The hummingbird is still
here stammering in my chest.

Icon of Panagia Faneromeni

I don't believe in Virgin birth
but something about this particular mother—
how she tilts her head toward the baby
never taking her eyes off me
a look so kind
in its fixed moment.
Her right hand gestures
across her torso to hold
the blessed infant's hand—
at least I think so—
the little reproduction I hold
somewhat fuzzy
simply paper glued on wood
an illusion to make it appear authentic.
In the movement, stillness.
In the silence
cacophony as my doubts arise—
wild and wayward
younger days, actions I've spent
years trying to reconcile
that I'd just as soon forget.
My own mother taught me to pray
to the Virgin Mary to beg forgiveness
but what did I know back then?
Panagia Faneromeni—Greek
for *Virgin Mary revealed.*

My mother had an icon
on her wall, the bodies of mother
and child covered in tarnished silver
to hide the portrait's erosion underneath
only the faces, the eyes, conspicuous.

The day Jack Gilbert kissed me

my father's grave was still fresh
and Mother alive.
The cemetery a kaleidoscope.

The dead asleep in the green field—
and I so awake and alive with Jack
standing on the remnants of bone
from which I was made.

When I say *kaleidoscope*
I mean the broken mirror
that reflects past my past.
I'm only guessing here.

Jack's lips a hot bloom pressed against mine
such uncontrollable collateral.

The sky a contronym
pounding above our heads, below our feet.

A mirage appeared—
and when I say *mirage*
I mean a scroll
raveled across the lawn
and placed its cloak of words.

A Dutch word—*ravelen,* loose thread—
rose up.

Isn't that what life in its overcoat
of mystery is all about?

The loose thread of an unexpected kiss
while laying flowers
at your father's grave.

All I can say is the sun—
I'm sure of this—
was a hot knife slicing

the air into before and after
that day Jack Gilbert kissed me.

It made me remember what I forgot—
that smell of summer—loamy, rich, wet—
brought up from the earth.

Reading George Kalogeris's Poems, I Remember My Mother's Grape Leaves

Mother plucks the heart-shaped green leaves
from the park's grapevine—
they darken limp over the plate.
Rice, pine nuts, onions and parsley mixed in a bowl—olive
oil,
salt and pepper and one more mystery ingredient
I still can't quite define.

How careful she is
trying not to tear her first leaf.
She spoons a mound
onto the middle of the vine's open palm.
Fingering each tapered point she pulls the lobes
toward the center, curls the bottom up
to roll a little log.

I want to speak.
Nothing spills.
She tiles the wall of her cast iron pot
repeating up the sides, four rolls deep
and leaves a hole in the middle—an empty space
that carries the weight of such work—

leaving room
for me to stay in the memory of her kitchen
to write out this mysticism of steam

leaving room
for a drinking glass to hold stuffed grape leaves
tight against their embankment—

My mother sat me down in the kitchen
repeating ancient Greek prayers in a tongue
sung only in church—*maker of heaven and earth*—

How the Greeks invented compound words
like *avgolemono*—bright egg-lemon sauce
that shines across the tongue
now poured over the taut coils.

She checks her stacks
to keep the soup
from curdling
to ensure each roll stays put.
Just like George's Greek mother—I'm certain of it.
She lowers the heat
to keep from burning
what's been made.

Portrait of Peter the Priest as Rhododendron

It hasn't been easy to think of you
now that you're gone, the afternoon light
aslant and rhododendron unbloomed.

You missed the trip to the doctor, you
feared the fire behind your eyes.
Almost impossible to think of who,

or what, you've become, under the slew
of winter's glisten, still and ice.
The rhododendron hides its bloom.

Your daughter's grief is soaking through
the empty house, turning off lights.
It's painful, really, to think of you.

And I, though not your daughter, askew
inside my body's house. The price
of mourning: the rhododendron's ruin.

Having lost what we lost when we lost you
how to spark lidless days and nights?
It hasn't been easy to remember you.
Roses, trees aslant, unbloomed.

Naming

I rolled in the awful stink of a ship's hold
to land, finally, on this country's soil.

For the intake officer, I tendered
my given name: Zerboulidis—*too long* he said.

I was a boy. I measured the rings of the family tree
with my footsteps.

My new name sibilant
in the new world—

Vassos—embedded
in granite

Loving Father and Husband
1907–2003

My daughter's feet over my coat of dirt—
what's that she's saying?

She bends to place the flowers she holds
to wipe pebbles from the stone.

I tell you this as if she can hear me.

Into the Shallows

A trick of the eye
transfigures nature into gold.

It was you, Mother,
who insisted
in your last, sad years

that the maples near the shore were so tall
& gloried
because their roots pulled water from the lake.

I keep looking
into the shallows.
I can almost see

the maker of your ring
tracing soft metal
cutting away what's extraneous—

how I coveted this ring—
& now that it's mine I don't want it.

I am rearranged by your gift
and you are dead.

Note to Self: Crow

Stand at the edge of a clearing
your hand curved at your brow
to keep out the sun.

Regard the crow's distance
calculated on the abacus of her wings.

Bow your head
the pen across the page.

Letter to the Driver of the White SUV That Killed a Crow

You scared the shit out of me.
Swerved so fast and close,
the wind you dragged displacing me.
Tell me how many times you've blown
past 60 in this 30-mph stretch.
It was you last week
when I was out riding my bicycle—
you in your two-ton, salt-stained vehicle.
You saw it too—that sleek, smart crow
once alive with squawk and fury
maybe a branch in its beak
as it lifted off the road
maybe making its way to build a nest—
now a pile of blood, feathers
mangled marrow
in the middle of the road.
Have you picked out the feathers
stuck in the cracks of your windshield?
Here at my desk
I hear the thump again
feel the jump
when you didn't slow down.

I can tell you how smart the glossy Corvus can be:
that crow could have picked you
out in a crowd, finagled a tool
to poke your eye out—
then flown to the nearest tree
to wait for you with his murder.

Love Poem with an Apology in the Middle

Hyperbole is something I don't believe in.
I'm sorry we will die one day.
The body I clothe is mine.
I wear you, unbuttoned.

Fragments

On my walk yesterday,
a scrap of letter
next to my shoe
                              on the sidewalk
caught my eye
it was torn
                    I made out fragments:
re mber lo e
                              oh such pleasure it is
to remember love
and every young man
I kissed in college
their long hair luminous, falling in their eyes—
that ringing in my ears
the rain.

October

The way light mutates
into glory
over my friend's shoulder—
we stop to face each other after our walk—
the sun's raucous afternoon
cascading into night's solemn basket.

The neighbor's beech tree
has laid her gold crown on the pavement.

My sweater, thrown over the back of the chair.

I'm not afraid
to be the last standing figure
in a stand of figures—
to touch the foreheads, the hands
of those I've loved
as they drift to their own ground—
I'm not afraid to be last.

I read a book once about how
when death comes
the glow is glorious, blinding.
Fifty years ago
I made love to a man
who loved someone else—
I loved him anyway.
As brilliant as that.

November

Leaves drip their red and orange puddles
on the grass. I drive west on Beacon Street.

November's sun glazes the clouds—
steel-gray bundles

that hold down the horizon
as if tethered by blue ribbon.

A garnet suture binds sky to earth.

From the car radio the trumpet strains
of "The Times of Harvey Milk" wander like smoke

seeking its unfiltered cigarette.
The music reaches into the round window

of my ear, squeezing as if my heart
could be found there. It's late.

I squint through the windshield at the road ahead,
at shredded remnants of this tenuous day.

If the sun makes a sound as it sets in November,
it is a trumpet, wailing.

In the Way

The sky clouded over
The day we rode the bike path at Bryce.
I was ahead, setting the pace, past the bristlecone pines—

On my right, a doe from nowhere
Bounded across my line, ran beside my bicycle.
Her fawn on the left—now a trio, racing

To get across the road, to the woods.
I was chosen. In the way.
We flew & I—feet pedaling & a thought, almost

Don't stop. Moving, hold
Your line.

Then, my sisters & almost-thoughts disappeared,
Each in different directions.

It was seconds, the other cyclists said.

Oh, but for me, time's slow
Motion. My breathing, my—
I slipped into the gap

Where air is thin & thick at once
A wilderness of feeling, of precision:

We were alone.
I held my line & flew.

25 Miles In, 10 to Go

The bike seat hard against my butt—wind slices
into my leggings, my gloves.
43 degrees. Feet cold despite wool socks and booties.

16 miles per hour and the wind
takes my flesh in its teeth
and doesn't let go.

20 years ago, that first summer
I clipped into pedals, certain I'd fall—
G, running beside me

in the parking lot
calling *I won't let you fall*
then letting me fall.

The silent breath of the world
opens throat, sudden—
whistles through my cochlea—a howl.

And Rilke's phrase an earworm:
what birds plunge through is not the intimate space.
I'm a knife, I cleave into the wind.

Cold rips through my jacket.
Caribbean trade winds
blow to mind—

my parents sitting in the sun.
Remembering the dead,
my quads burn.

The bike seat rough. Pussy Riot's endless loop:
Does your vagina
Let your vagina

Pedal strokes stuttering uphill
out-of-control slipping downhill
trying not to coast.

G insists on *perfect circles—*
pedal, pedal, pedal, it's all about cadence.
OK Coach, I gasp to keep up

latching onto his wheel to draft
hammering through the hills as we enter Concord
feet frozen, my vulva burning.

Note to Self: Other Side

You measure
a length of beach
moved by wind
your long slow strides.
Will it break you?

You are the long slow beast.

You know this:
                    it arrives on the other side of difficulty.

When I say *it,* I mean
this poem.
I mean
the flame inside you.

Persephone's Plaint to Demeter

I can't stop eating.
I'll show you how to disrobe
a pomegranate.

Soon the meadow
will be a white sheet

waiting for my body's imprint.
Call me Queen, and flame.
Call me predicate, and subject.

I Remember My Dream While Listening to My Teacher Read "Rain, New Year's Eve"

Her hand a verb.
She could grab
a fly in flight
if she wanted.

Now, blue light glows
through my computer screen
she greets me
hello, friend—
and reads the Maggie Smith poem twice
while her palm, for emphasis
sweeps across the screen—
and though I have the book
I can't locate the poem.

I don't care.
I remember instead
what I dreamed—
when eyes, bankrupt to the world
watched phosphenes swirling—

I walked the cobbles of San Miguel de Allende
looking for my teacher
the roof dogs whimpering
above the buildings
the jacaranda sweeping down.

This talk of rain on New Year's Eve—
how I do love the world, too.

But it's the middle of September
before fall even begins—
the days still glow hot.
Earliest light streaks the window,
ignites my own hand as I meet
myself on this page.

How I Become Bilingual

Father almighty
Mother recited

I repeated
Πατερα παντοκράτορα—

one sound at a time
word by word

heard & repeated:
Maker of heaven & earth

cadences the way
Homer might have sung them:

Ποιητην ουρανού και γης—
woven into the sinew

of my eight-year-old body
as Mother ironed

every fabric
washed clean that morning:

bed sheets
underwear, Father's handkerchiefs.

Tonight, I bend over the laptop—
the lamp's skirt

illuminates the prayer's
Greek letters.

One word for God
and laundry done.

song for Peter the Priest who sang before he died

where flung
my friend
now what
earth swallows
where flown
thrice-holy: *trisagion*
lose losing lost
kyrie eleison
mouth full of feathers
gasp full of what
echo of gasp
echo of echo
your throat
full of birds
their songs like gospels
gospels sung
kissed to earth
bed-hurt mud
bedrock dirt
dust of your shoe
gone did you go
tenor to hold
art thou in heaven
now full of flown
now swallowed
now swallow
now what

Letter from Inside My Name

In Greek, friend, Anastasia
translates to *resurrection—*
I know you didn't know that.
Though your mother was cruel
you are the kindest person I know—
you yourself so in need of kindness.
Yesterday, three daffodils
blossomed in front of the house
and though it will take another two
months for the rhododendron
I'll practice patience and let you know
when her purple flowers flourish
the air around her. Did you know
rhodo/dendron translates
to *rose/tree?* I don't know why
I've never told you about my own
mother's toughness as I grew up.
Her gift of language, the *glossa*
of the Greeks made it endurable.
Did you know that *glossa* means
tongue? The root of the word
glossary, glossolalia. It's almost
Easter, and my name nods
to the resurrection of Christ
whether you and I believe in that or not.
I like to think of myself as a power
rising out of a shadow-cave to sunlight, renewal.
There is a coin. There are two sides.
My mother never stopped

loving me and I have never stopped
loving her. I bury disappointment
under my tongue.
Pretty soon it will be the tulips' turn—
and yesterday, kind Dr. Wang scraped
away layers of my husband's skin
before the roots of *melanoma*
(from Greek *blackness*) dug in.

Thessaloniki, 1970

On Egnatia Street
a boy balances
his copper tray
of Greek coffee
for the old tailor
dressed in black.
This city’s love
stitches the quiet
fabric of my bones.

*

Just so. Inside the Church
of Agios Demetrios
a priest casts
his rounded censor
held by three
delicate chains.
Alone there
his prayers ascend.

*

Meltemi winds appear
the way faith appears
unrelenting. The sea
beside the taverna
could drown me
if I let it.
On picnic tables
sand scatters
like salt.

Nepenthe

Tasso's olive oil from Athikia
sits in shipping containers
on the dock in South Boston.

He's pressed the oil himself, mallet aimed at the shiny flesh
of Kalamata fruit, olives that wept to earth
postage-stamp shade of the tree.

It's freezing here. The storm that covered us
in snow moves out off the Atlantic,
the ocean I love best—
though I once stepped into the Aegean's vowels
and can't forget

my ancestors
ancient cursive
my mother's hand and homeland
Tasso squeezing the sun
out of the olives—
and on the wind
a scent of licorice.

Note to Self: Mighty Oak

The dead are not gone.
Allow this: rest
in uncertainty—
the low-slung hammock
between two oaks.

In Which I Talk to Ralph About the Afterlife

Your belief in God so firm
it was on the high shelf
I could not reach.

In the hospice room you said
health isn't the most important thing.
It's love.

You organized your books
read on the back porch
listening to Mahler.

Love is not a fungible word.

There's a raven
croaking every time
I sit down to write.

You would have loved all that.

At Mount Athos

The tourist boat slows past Mount Athos.
The Greek over the intercom so garbled
I think I don't know Greek.

We watch hermits
locked by faith on the mountain
release baskets down
on frayed ropes for the bread we offer.
For water.

What do they cling to?
How is time measured on a holy bluff?

I push my way
through the throng to the bow
where a priest has boarded—
head to toe in black
in this sweltering—

he opens a silver reliquary
a saint's relics inside. Bones
barely visible that appear burnt
like charcoal
if they are, in fact, bones.

My Ilion

How does one outlive regret? Is it like trying to evade
one's skin? Or peeling back an onion's petals until reaching
the root, one chucks it all in compost so it can live again?

I've never been one for staying put—a hummingbird
in my chest bangs about, looking for its way home.
It feels like a china shop in there, a bull the size of an insect.

Tell me how many fingers I'm holding up. Describe the distance
between *there* and *here.* When Achilles strutted the length
of Ilion's beach, he held his troops in thrall, unwavering

in his pride. My own frailty resides—not in the back of my ankle—
but in my heart's dark corner, refusing love over and over.
What is the distance between the heel and the heart in that scenario?

Thomas Merton called one's refusal to accept love *the pattern*
and prototype of all sin. When I was small I thought sin was eating
a turkey sandwich on Good Friday instead of fasting for communion.

Look: was I loved too much? When is enough enough? Downtown,
I tripped on a crack in the sidewalk and had to think through
how I'd rise from the fall while a family of strangers

surrounded me, offering help. Oh, I denied them that, my
hubris
and bones intact. I don't want to outlive anything. I want
to *in-live*
—to remember, to enter my body's scrapes, how morning
gallops

across the city's sidewalks, chasing night. Infinite web.
Infinitive.
To let myself settle within the thin confines of skin, to spill ink
into the arms of the page, to submerge in flight: my consort,
my love.

Notes

"Garden State"—for Raymond Koeppel

"Rolling Prairie"—last line borrowed from Sarah Dickenson Snyder

"Standing in Line at the Post Office, I Want to Mail My Book to My Dead Mother"—for Eileen Cleary

"Letter to Peter the Priest as He Awaits the Day of Judgment," "Portrait of Peter the Priest as Rhododendron," "song for Peter the Priest who sang before he died"—in memory of Reverend Peter Metallinos

"It Could Be Any Day, Say, January 11"—after Hayden Carruth

"Lake Waban"—for the Montebello group, and in memory of Patrice Martin

"A Poet Goes About Her Business"—the title is also the title of a Linda Gregg poem

"October"—in memory of Laura Paul Watson

"25 Miles In, 10 to Go"—the Rilke phrase *what birds plunge through is not the intimate space* is quoted from a lecture by Anne Carson at MFA Boston in 2023 titled "Rustle of Catullus." In that lecture she also referenced a lyric by Pussy Riot.

“Note to Self: Other Side”—the line “[it] arrives on the other side of difficulty” is paraphrased from a Chris Abani discussion on elegy with Ellen Bass

“I Remember My Dream While Listening to My Teacher Read *Rain, New Year’s Eve*”—for Laurie Wagner

“Letter from Inside My Name”—for Phyllis Klein

“In Which I Talk to Ralph About the Afterlife”—in memory of Ralph Donaldson

About the Author

Anastasia Vassos, the daughter of Greek immigrants, was born in Cleveland, Ohio. Her poems have been nominated for the Pushcart Prize, Best of the Net, and Best New Poets. She is the author of the chapbook *Nostos* (Kelsay Books, 2023) and *Nike Adjusting Her Sandal* (Nixes Mate, 2021). Her poems about the Greek-American experience have been translated into Greek. She is a reader for Lily Poetry Review, speaks three languages, and lives in Boston.

www.ingramcontent.com/pod-product-compliance
Lightning Source LLC
LaVergne TN
LVHW090534110826
845146LV00003B/1094

* 9 7 9 8 9 0 1 4 6 8 5 1 7 *